Interview Questions

You'll Most Likely Be Asked

Job Interview Questions Series

www.vibrantpublishers.com

Software Testing Interview Questions
You'll Most Likely Be Asked

ISBN-10: 1456579304
ISBN-13: 978-14-56579-30-2

Library of Congress Control Number: 2011921651

The publisher wishes to thank Dana Mitrea (Romania) for her invaluable inputs to this edition.

Please email feedback / corrections (technical, grammatical or spelling) to **spellerrors@vibrantpublishers.com**

To access the complete catalogue of Vibrant Publishers, visit **www.vibrantpublishers.com**

Contents

This page is intentionally left blank

Software Testing Questions

Review these typical interview questions and think about how you would answer them. Read the answers listed; you will find best possible answers along with strategies and suggestions.

This page is intentionally left blank

General Testing Concepts

1: Why is testing necessary?

Answer:

Testing is necessary not only in order to find bugs, but also:

a) To improve the quality of the product
b) To decrease the rate of failures (increase the product's reliability)
c) To ensure that the requirements are implemented fully and correctly
d) To validate that the product is fit for its intended purpose
e) To verify that the required standards and legal requirements are met

2: Can a product be 100% tested?

Answer:

Exhaustive testing is impossible. Instead, there must be understood the risk to the client's business of the software not functioning correct. This can be done by carrying out a Risk Analysis of the application and prioritising tests - they must be focused on the main areas of risk.

3: What are the main goals of testing?

Answer:

The main goals of testing are:

a) To find defects
b) To assess the level of quality of the software product

and providing related information to the stakeholders

c) To prevent defects
d) To reduce risk of operational incidents
e) To increase the product quality

4: What is quality assurance?

Answer:

Quality assurance, or QA for short, is the systematic monitoring and evaluation of the various aspects of a project, service or facility to maximize the probability that minimum standards of quality are being attained by the production process. QA cannot absolutely guarantee the production of quality products.

5: What are the two principle of quality assurance?

Answer:

The two principles included in QA are:

a) "Fit for purpose" - the product should be suitable for the intended purpose
b) "Right first time" - mistakes should be eliminated.

6: What is the difference between quality assurance and testing?

Answer:

Quality assurance involves the entire software development process and testing involves operation of a system or application to evaluate the results under certain conditions. QA is oriented to prevention and testing is oriented to detection.

7: What is a defect (or a bug)?

Answer:

A defect (or a bug) is a flaw that can cause the component or system to fail to perform its required function. Not all software defects are caused by coding errors. One common source of expensive defects is caused by requirement gaps, e.g. unrecognized requirements that result in errors of omission by the program designer.

8: What is a failure?

Answer:

A failure is deviation of the component or system from its expected delivery, service or result.

9: What in an anomaly?

Answer:

An anomaly represents any condition that deviates from expectations based on requirements specifications, design documents/ user documentation/ standards or someone's perceptions or expectations.

10: What is defect masking? What are its consequences?

Answer:

Defect masking is an occurrence in which one defect prevents the detection of another. It can lead to difficulties in finding the root cause of a problem.

11: What are the root causes of defects?

Answer:

Defects are caused by human errors. Reasons that lead to errors might be:

a) Time pressure - the more pressure we are under the more likely we are to make mistakes
b) Code complexity or new technology
c) Too many system interactions
d) Poor training
e) Poor communication
f) Requirements not clearly defined, changed or not properly documented

12: Which are the criteria used to decide when to stop testing?

Answer:

The five basic criteria often used to decide when to stop testing are:

a) Previously defined coverage goals have been met
b) The defect discovery rate has dropped below a previously defined threshold
c) The cost of finding the "next" defect exceeds the expected loss from that defect

d) The project team reaches consensus that it is appropriate to release the product
e) The manager decides to deliver the product

13: What is testing activity?

Answer:

Testing activity is the process concerned with planning the necessary static and dynamic activities, preparation and evaluation of software products and related deliverables, in order to:

a) Determine that they satisfy specified requirements
b) Demonstrate that they are fit for the intended use
c) Detect defects, help and motivate the developers to fix them
d) Measure, assess and improve the quality of the software product

14: Give example of several best practices in requirements based testing.

Answer:

Requirements-based testing process addresses two major issues: first, validating that the requirements are correct, complete, unambiguous, and logically consistent; and second, designing a necessary and sufficient (from a black box perspective) set of test cases from those requirements to ensure that the design and code fully meet those requirements. Several best practices would be:

a) Validate requirements (what) against objectives (why)
b) Apply use cases against requirements
c) Perform ambiguity reviews
d) Involve domain experts in requirements reviews
e) Create cause-effect diagrams
f) Check logical consistency of test scenarios
g) Validate test scenarios with domain experts and users
h) Walk through scenarios comparing with design documents
i) Walk through scenarios comparing with code

15: What are the steps that need to be performed in order to create good test scenarios?

Answer:

Below are describes several steps that need to be followed in order to have good test scenarios:

a) Write down real-life stories
b) List possible users, analyze their interests and objectives
c) Consider also inexperienced or hostile users
d) List system benefits and create paths to access those features
e) Watch users using old versions of the system or an analog system
f) Study complaints about other analog systems

16: Which is the Pareto rule (defect clustering rule)?

Answer:

Pareto rule states that usually 20% of the modules contain 80% of the bugs.

17: Which persons have the testers to interact with during the testing cycles?

Answer:

In order to implement a good testing strategy, testers cooperate with:

a) Analysts – to review the specifications for completeness and correctness, ensure that they are testable
b) Designers – to improve interfaces testability and usability
c) Programmers – to review the code and assess structural flaws
d) Project manager – to estimate, plan, develop test cases, perform tests and report bugs, to assess the quality and risks
e) Other quality assurance staff – to provide defect metrics

18: What are the factors that measure product quality?

Answer:

Product quality can be measured through a variety of factors like:

a) Functional compliance - functional software

requirements testing

b) Non functional requirements like security, performance, usability, manageability
c) Test coverage criteria
d) Defect count or defect trend criteria

19: What is a test Oracle?

Answer:

A test Oracle is a source to determine expected result, a principle or mechanism to recognize a problem. The Test Oracle can be:

a) An existing system (for example/ the old version…)
b) A document (specification, user manual)
c) A competent client representative

20: Which conditions have to be met such that the source code could be considered a test Oracle?

Answer:

The source code itself can never be considered a test Oracle.

21: What is the difference between verification and validation?

Answer:

Verification checks that the thing is done right while validation checks that the right thing is done.

22: Provide a short definition of reliability. How is reliability measured?

Answer:

Reliability represents the ability of a software product to perform its required functions under stated conditions for a specified period of time, or for a specified number of operations. Reliability is not measured, it is estimated.

23: What is the usability of an application?

Answer:

Usability represents the capability of the software to be understood, learned, used and attractive to the user when used under specified conditions.

24: Which are the main levels of testing?

Answer:

There are four main levels of testing:

a) Unit testing (also known as Component level testing)
b) Integration Testing
c) System Testing
d) Acceptance Testing

25: What would be the psychological characteristics of a good tester?

Answer:

A good tester:

a) Should always have a critical approach
b) Must keep attention to detail
c) Should have good verbal and written communication skills
d) Must analyze and work with incomplete facts
e) Must learn quickly about the product being tested
f) Should be able to quickly prioritize
g) Should be a planned, organized kind of person
h) Must have a good knowledge about the customer's business workflows, the product architecture and interfaces, the software project process

26: What are the levels of independence of the testing team?

Answer:

There are three main levels of independence of a testing team:

a) Low – Developers write and execute their own tests
b) Medium – Tests are written and executed by another developer
c) High – Tests written and executed by an independent testing team (internal or external)

27: What is a test case?

Answer:

A test case is a set of input values, execution preconditions, expected results and execution post-conditions, developed for a particular objective or test condition, such as to exercise a particular program path or to verify compliance with a specific requirement.

28: What is a test condition?

Answer:

A test condition is an item, event, attribute of a module or system that could be verified (ex: feature, structure element, transaction, quality attribute)

29: What is extreme programming? What is the relation between extreme programming and testing?

Answer:

Extreme programming is a software development approach for small teams on risk-prone projects with unstable requirements. Testing is a core aspect of Extreme Programming. Programmers are expected to write unit and functional test code first - before the application is developed. Test code is under source control along with the rest of the code. Acceptance tests are preferably automated, and are modified and rerun for each of the frequent development iterations. QA and test personnel are also required to be an integral part of the project team. Detailed requirements documentation is not used, and frequent re-scheduling, re-estimating, and re-prioritizing is expected.

Testing Phases

30: What are the steps performed during test development process?

Answer:

Test development process involves three main phases:

a) Identify test conditions - by inputs, capability and architectural design
b) Develop test cases - test cases are developed based on use cases and should cover all possible paths of the execution graph flow
c) Develop test procedures - grouping test cases into execution schedules, performing risk analysis

31: Which are the main testing phases?

Answer:

The main testing phases are the following:

a) Test Planning & Test control
b) Test Analysis & Design
c) Test Implementation & Execution
d) Evaluating exit criteria & Reporting
e) Test Closure activities

32: What is a test plan?

Answer:

A test plan is a document describing the scope, approach, resources and schedule of intended test activities. It identifies amongst others test items, the features to be tested, the testing tasks, who will do each task, degree of tester independence, the test environment, the test design techniques and test measurement techniques to be used, and the rationale for their choice, and any risks requiring contingency planning.

33: Which are the phases of test planning?

Answer:

Test planning phases are the following:

a) Determine scope - Study project documents, used software life-cycle specifications, product desired quality attributes, clarify test process expectations
b) Determine risks - Choose quality risk analysis method, document the list of risks, probability, impact, priority, identify mitigation actions
c) Estimate testing effort, determine costs, develop schedule, define necessary roles, decompose test project into phases and tasks, schedule tasks, assign resources, set-up dependencies
d) Refine plan - Select test strategy, select metrics to be used for defect tracking, coverage, monitoring, define entry and exit criteria

34: What tasks are implemented through test control?

Answer:

Test control implies execution of the following tasks:

a) Measuring and analyzing results

b) Monitoring testing progress, coverage, exit criteria
c) Assigning or reallocating resources, update the test plan schedule
d) Initiating corrective actions
e) Making decisions

35: Which factors must be taken into account when choosing a specific testing technique?

Answer:

Factors used to choose between different testing techniques are:

a) Product or system type
b) Standards
c) Product's requirements
d) Available documentation
e) Determined risks
f) Schedule constraints
g) Cost constraints
h) Used software development life cycle model
i) Tester's skills and (domain) experience

36: Which are the steps that need to be performed during test implementation?

Answer:

Test implementation activity follows the steps below:

a) Develop and prioritize test cases, create test data, test harnesses and automation scripts

b) Create test suites from the test cases

c) Check test environment

37: What are the activities performed during test execution?

Answer:

Test execution implies the following activities:

a) Executing (manually or automatically) the test cases (suites)

b) Using Test Oracles to determine if the tests passed or failed

c) Login the outcome of tests execution

d) Report incidents (bugs) and try to discover if they are caused by the test data, test procedure or they are defect failures

38: What are the reasons to prioritize the test cases?

Answer:

Test cases must be prioritized because:

a) It is not possible to test everything, we must do our best in the time available

b) Testing must be Risk based, assuring that the errors, that will get through to the client's production system/ will have the smallest possible impact and frequency of occurrence

39: Give example of several test cases prioritization criteria:

Answer:

Test cases can be prioritized upon the following criteria:

a) Severity of possible defects
b) Probability of possible defects
c) Visibility of possible defects
d) Client Requirement importance
e) Business or technical criticality of a feature
f) Frequency of changes applied to a module
g) Scenarios complexity

40: What needs to be taken into account when evaluating the exit criteria?

Answer:

Exit criteria are evaluated through the following points of view:

a) Check test logs against exit criteria specified in test mission definition
b) Assess if more tests are needed
c) Check if testing mission should be changed

41: What should include a test summary report?

Answer:

A test summary report should include:

a) Test Cases execution coverage (% executed)
b) Test Cases Pass / Fail %
c) Active bugs, sorted according to their severity

42: What are the processes implemented during test closure activity?

Answer:

Test closure activity implies the following processes:

a) Verify if test deliverables have been delivered
b) Check and close the remaining active bug reports
c) Archiving the test-ware and environment
d) Handover of the test environment
e) Analyze the identified test process problems (lessons learned)
f) Implement action plan based improvements

43: Give examples of several best practices in preparing manual test scripts.

Answer:

When preparing manual test scripts it is a good option to take into account the following best practices:

a) Test only one condition in each test case
b) Include a question at the end of each test case which should be verification point
c) The expected answer to that question will be expected result.
d) The status (pass/fail) of the test cases should be evaluated by the answer to that question
e) Test cases should descriptive.

Types Of Testing

44: What is verification? In which testing levels is it most used?

Answer:

Verification is the confirmation by examination and through the provision of objective evidence that specified requirements have been fulfilled. It is is the dominant activity in the unit, integration, system testing levels.

45: What is validation? In which testing levels is it most used?

Answer:

Validation is the confirmation by examination and through provision of objective evidence that the requirements for a specific intended use or application have been fulfilled. It is a mandatory activity in the acceptance testing level.

46: What is unit testing? By whom is it usually performed?

Answer:

Unit testing is a method by which individual units of source code are tested to determine if they are fit for use. A unit is the smallest testable part of an application. Unit testing is usually performed by the developers and occasionally by white box testers.

47: What are the benefits offered by unit testing?

Answer:

Unit testing provides a strict, written contract that the piece of code must satisfy. Several benefits of unit testing are:

a) It facilitates change - allows the programmer to refactor code at a later date, and make sure the module still works correctly
b) It simplifies integration - by testing the parts of a program first and then testing the sum of its parts, integration testing becomes much easier
c) Documentation - unit testing provides a sort of living documentation of the system

48: What is integration testing?

Answer:

Integration testing is the phase in software testing in which individual software modules are combined and tested as a group. It takes as its input modules that have been unit tested, groups them in larger aggregates, applies tests defined in an integration test plan to those aggregates, and delivers as its output the integrated system ready for system testing.

49: What are the integration testing strategies?

Answer:

There are three integration testing strategies:

a) Bottom-up - is an approach to integrated testing where the lowest level components are tested first, then used to facilitate the testing of higher level components.-

b) Top-down - is an approach to integrated testing where the top integrated modules are tested and the branch of the module is tested step by step until the end of the related module.

c) Big-Bang - in this approach, all or most of the developed modules are coupled together to form a complete software system or major part of the system and then used for integration testing.

50: What is a driver? In which type of testing is it used?

Answer:

A driver is a software component or test tool that replaces a component that takes care of the control and/or the calling of a component or system. It is used usually in top-down integration testing.

51: What is a stub? In which type of testing is it used?

Answer:

A stub is skeletal or special-purpose implementation of a software component, used to develop or test a component that calls or is otherwise dependent on it. It replaces a called component. It is used in bottom-up integration testing.

52: What is system testing?

Answer:

System testing is the process of testing an integrated system to verify that it meets specified requirements. It targets the whole product as defined in the scope document and may consist of:

a) Functional tests, based on the requirement specifications
b) Non-functional tests
c) Structural tests

53: What is acceptance testing?

Answer:

Acceptance testing is a formal testing with respect to user needs, requirements, and business processes conducted to determine whether or not a system satisfies the acceptance criteria and to enable the user, customers or other authorized entity to determine whether or not to accept the system. It may be executed also after component testing and usually involves client representatives.

54: Which are the main goals of acceptance testing?

Answer:

The main focus of acceptance testing is not to find defects, but to assess the readiness for deployment. Other goals would be:

a) To establish confidence in the system
b) To decide if the product is good enough to be delivered to the client

55: Which are the typical forms of acceptance testing?

Answer:

The typical forms of acceptance testing are the following:

a) User acceptance - business aware users verify the main features
b) Operational acceptance testing - backup-restore, security, maintenance
c) Alpha and Beta testing - performed by customers or potential users

56: Which is the difference between Alpha and Beta testing?

Answer:

Alpha testing is performed at the developer's site while Beta testing is performed at the customer's site.

57: What is functional testing?

Answer:

Functional testing is a type of black box testing that checks the system against the specifications. A product's specification is based on:

a) Test Cases, derived from use cases
b) Business scenarios

58: What is non-functional testing? Give several examples.

Answer:

Non functional testing is the process of testing the attributes of a component or system that do not relate to functionality.

Examples of non-functional types of testing would be:

a) Performance testing
b) Load testing (how much load can be handled by the system?)
c) Stress testing (evaluate system behavior at limits and out of limits)
d) Usability testing
e) Reliability testing
f) Portability testing
g) Maintainability testing

59: What is usability testing?

Answer:

Usability testing is a type of testing used to determine the extent to which the software product is understood, easy to learn, easy to operate and attractive to the users under specified conditions.

60: What is installability testing?

Answer:

Installability testing is the process of testing the installability of a software product. It answers to several questions like:

a) Does the installation work?
b) How easy is to install the system?
c) Does installation affect other software?
d) Does the environment affect the product?

e) Does it uninstall correctly?

61: What is load testing?

Answer:

Load testing is a test type concerned with measuring the behavior of a component or system with increasing load, e.g. number of parallel users and/or numbers of transactions to determine what load can be handled by the component or system.

62: What is the difference between stress testing and performance testing?

Answer:

Stress testing is conducted to evaluate a system or component at or beyond the limits of its specified requirements while performance testing determines the performance of a software product.

63: What is performance testing? Which are its sub-genres?

Answer:

Performance testing is the type of testing that is performed in order to determine how fast some aspect of a system performs under a particular workload. It has the following sub-genres:

a) Load Testing
b) Stress Testing
c) Endurance Testing (Soak Testing)

d) Spike Testing
e) Configuration Testing
f) Isolation Testing

64: Which are the activities involved by performance testing?

Answer:

The activities involved in performance testing are the following:

a) Identify the test environment - hardware, software, network configurations
b) Identify performance acceptance criteria - the response time, throughput, and resource utilization goals and constraints
c) Plan and design tests - identify key scenarios, determine variability among representative users and how to simulate that variability, define test data, and establish metrics to be collected
d) Configure the test environment - prepare the test environment, tools, and resources necessary to execute the tests
e) Implement the test design - develop the performance tests in accordance with the test design
f) Execute the Test. Run and monitor your tests. Validate the tests, test data, and results collection. Execute validated tests for analysis while monitoring the test and the test environment.

g) Analyze Results, Tune, and Retest.

65: Give several reasons why stress testing is necessary.

Answer:

Stress testing is necessary if:

a) The software being tested is "mission critical", that is, failure of the software (such as a crash) would have disastrous consequences.
b) The amount of time and resources dedicated to testing is usually not sufficient, with traditional testing methods, to test all of the situations in which the software will be used when it is released.
c) Even with sufficient time and resources for writing tests, it may not be possible to determine beforehand all of the different ways in which the software will be used.
d) Customers may use the software on computers that have significantly fewer computational resources (such as memory or disk space) than the computers used for testing.
e) Concurrency is particularly difficult to test with traditional testing methods. Stress testing may be necessary to find race conditions and deadlocks.
f) Software such as web servers that will be accessible over the Internet may be subject to denial of service attacks.
g) Under normal conditions, certain types of bugs, such as

memory leaks, can be fairly benign and difficult to detect over the short periods of time in which testing is performed. However, these bugs can still be potentially serious. In a sense, stress testing for a relatively short period of time can be seen as simulating normal operation for a longer period of time.

66: Which is the relationship between stress testing and branch coverage?

Answer:

Stress testing can achieve higher branch coverage by producing the conditions under which certain error handling branches are followed. The coverage can be further improved by using fault injection. Example: a web server may be stress tested using scripts, bots, and various denial of service tools to observe the performance of a web site during peak loads.

67: What is structural testing?

Answer:

Structural testing is a white box testing technique which is targeted to test the internal structure of a component and also the whole system architecture. It can be performed at all test levels and may be used also to help measure the test coverage (% of items being covered by tests).

68: What is confirmation testing?

Answer:

Confirmation testing means re-testing a module or product, to confirm that the previously detected defect was fixed. It implies the use of a bug tracking tool.

69: What is the difference between confirmation testing and debugging?

Answer:

Confirmation testing is an activity performed by the quality assurance team in order to check if a detected defect was fixed while debugging is a development activity consisting in finding the root cause of a problem and providing a fix for it.

70: What is regression testing?

Answer:

Regression testing means re-testing of a previously tested program following modification to ensure that new defects have not been introduced or uncovered as a result of the changes made. It is performed when the software or its environment is changed. It can be performed at all test levels and can be easily automated.

71: Define maintenance testing and give example of some operations included into it.

Answer:

Maintenance testing means testing the changes to an

operational system or the impact of a changed environment to an operational system. It is done on an existing operational system, triggered by modification, retirement or migration of the software and includes:

a) Release based changes
b) Corrective changes
c) Database upgrades

72: Describe equivalence partitioning testing technique. Provide a short example.

Answer:

Equivalence partitioning testing technique consists in partitioning the input (output) values into groups of equivalent values (equivalent from the test outcome perspective) and then select a value from each equivalence class as a representative value. As an example, if we have a software program that manages employments and the rule for hiring a person regarding its age is:

0 – 15 = do not hire

16 – 17 = part time

18 – 54 = full time

55 - 99 = do not hire

Then the representative values that might be chosen are included into these partitions (e.g. 7, 16, 21, 60)

73: What is all-pairs testing (or pairwise testing)?

Answer:

All-pairs testing is a combinatorial software testing method that, for each pair of input parameters to a system (typically, a software algorithm), tests all possible discrete combinations of those parameters. The reasoning behind all-pairs testing is that the simplest bugs in a program are generally triggered by a single input parameter. The next simplest category of bugs consists of those dependent on interactions between pairs of parameters, which can be caught with all-pairs testing.

74: Describe boundary value analysis technique. Provide a short example.

Answer:

Boundary value analysis is a software testing technique in which tests are designed to include representatives of boundary values. The values could be either input or output ranges of a software component. Since these boundaries are common locations for errors that result in software faults they are frequently exercised in test cases. For example, if we have to do a boundary value analysis for a range between 10-20, the values that should be tested would be:

(9,10,11) = (min-1, min, min+1) and (19,20,21) = (max-1, max, max+1)

75: What is context-driven testing?

Answer:

Context-driven testing is a paradigm for developing and debugging computer software that takes into account the ways in which the programs will be used or are expected to be used in the real world. It is sometimes considered a 'flavor' of agile software development.

76: What is conversion testing?

Answer:

Conversion testing is the procedure of testing programs (procedures) which is used to convert data from existing systems to data that will be used in the replacement systems.

77: What is destructive software testing?

Answer:

Destructive software testing is a type of software testing which attempts to cause a piece of software to fail in an uncontrolled manner, in order to test its robustness. It is similar to negative testing.

78: What is dependency testing?

Answer:

Dependency testing is a testing type which examines an application's requirements for pre-existing software, initial states and configuration in order to maintain proper functionality.

79: What is dynamic testing? Give example of several dynamic testing methodologies.

Answer:

Dynamic testing refers to the examination of the physical response from the system to variables that are not constant and change with time. In dynamic testing the software must actually be compiled and run; it involves working with the software, giving input values and checking if the output is as expected. Unit, integration, system and acceptance testing are several dynamic testing methodologies.

80: What is domain testing?

Answer:

Domain testing is a white box testing method whose goal is to check values taken by a variable, a condition, or an index, and to prove that they are outside the specified or valid range. It also contains checking that the program accepts only valid input, because it is unlikely to get reasonable results if idiocy has been entered. It covers the following statements:

a) Have all variables used been initialized correctly?
b) Are all indices used to access an array inside the array's dimensions?
c) Are all those indices integers?
d) Are all arguments in a comparison of the same type?
e) Are all boolean expressions correct? Check logical operands like AND, and OR, and their priorities.

f) Are there any 'off by one' situations, like a loop which is executed too often, or a field index of an array which is increased by one?

81: What is error-handling testing?

Answer:

Error-handling testing is software testing type which determines the ability of the system to properly process erroneous transactions.

82: What is end to end testing?

Answer:

End-to-end testing is the process of testing transactions or business level products as they pass right through the computer systems. Thus this generally ensures that all aspects of the business are supported by the systems under test. End-to-end testing ensures that the overall process flows as expected, that is that system components integrate together correctly and that the right information is passed between them.

83: What is fuzz testing?

Answer:

Fuzz testing or fuzzing is a software testing technique that provides invalid, unexpected, or random data to the inputs of a program. If the program fails (for example, by crashing or failing built-in code assertions), the defects can be noted. File formats and network protocols are the most common targets of fuzz testing, but any type of program input can be fuzzed.

84: Which are the types of bugs found through fuzz testing?

Answer:

Fuzz testing helps in finding several types of errors, like:

a) Straight-up failures - crashes, assertion failures, and memory leaks
b) Memory safety failures
c) Error-handling routines failures - since fuzzing often generates invalid input
d) Incorrect-serialization bugs - by complaining whenever a program's serializer emits something that the same program's parser rejects
e) Unintentional differences between two versions of a program or between two implementations of the same specification.

85: What is gray box testing?

Answer:

Gray box testing is a combination of black box and white box testing methodologies: it tests a piece of software against its specification but using some knowledge of its internal workings. Grey box testing may also include reverse engineering to determine, for instance, boundary values or error messages.

86: What is the goal of globalization testing?

Answer:

The goal of globalization testing is to detect potential problems in application design that could inhibit globalization. It makes sure that the code can handle all international support without breaking functionality that would cause either data loss or display problems. It checks proper functionality of the product with any of the culture/locale settings using every type of international input possible.

87: What type of tests does globalization testing include?

Answer:

Globalization Testing includes tests for:

a) System locale settings
b) System Locale
c) User Locale
d) Input Locale
e) Location or Geographic ID
f) UI Language
g) Browser locale settings
h) Identifying the culture/locale that must be supported
i) Character classification
j) Date and time formatting
k) Numeric, currency, and measure conventions

l) Sorting rules

88: What is internationalization testing?

Answer:

Internationalization 'I18n' refers to the process of designing, developing and engineering the product that can be adaptable to various locales and regions without further any engineering changes. Internationalization testing is the process which ensures that product's functionality is not broken and all the messages are properly externalized when used in different languages and locale.

89: Which are the tasks involved by internationalization process?

Answer:

I18n process typically involves the following tasks:

a) Externalizing of strings, graphics, icons, texts etc
b) Selecting code page and defining code page conversions
c) Modifying all the text manipulation functions to be aware of the code page
d) Changing the logic of all the formatting functions (Date, Time, Currency, Numeric, etc)
e) Changing the Collation /sorting functions

90: What is localization testing?

Answer:

Localization testing is part of software testing process focused on adapting a globalized application to a particular culture/locale. It includes translating the program, choosing the appropriate icons and graphics and other cultural considerations. It also may include the translation of help files and documentation.

91: What is inter-system testing?

Answer:

Inter-System Testing is a technique which tests the application to ensure interconnection between application functions correctly. It does the following:

a) Determine proper parameters and data are correctly passed between the applications
b) Documentation for involved system is correct and accurate.
c) Ensure proper timing and coordination of functions exists between the application systems.

92: What is loop testing?

Answer:

Loop testing is a white-box testing technique that focuses exclusively on the validity of loop constructs. There are four different classes of loops:

a) Simple loops
b) Concatenated loops

c) Nested loops
d) Unstructured loops

93: What is accessibility testing?

Answer:

Accessibility testing is the technique of making sure that a software product is accessibility compliant. Typical accessibility problems can be classified into following four groups:

a) Visual impairments - blindness, low or restricted vision, or color blindness
b) Motor skills - the inability to use a keyboard or mouse, or to make fine movements.
c) Hearing impairments - reduced or total loss of hearing
d) Cognitive abilities - reading difficulties, dyslexia or memory loss.

94: Give examples of some typical test cases for accessibility testing.

Answer:

Typical test cases for accessibility might look similar to the following examples:

a) Make sure that all functions are available via keyboard only (do not use mouse)
b) Make sure that information is visible when display setting is changed to High Contrast modes.

c) Make sure that screen reading tools can read all the text available and every picture/Image have corresponding alternate text associated with it.

d) Make sure that product defined keyboard actions do not affect accessibility keyboard shortcuts.

95: What is the difference between active and passive testing?

Answer:

Active testing involves a human mind while passive testing is merely following a previously laid out plan, probably with test scripts and test cases paved all the way. In active testing you build a mental model of the underlying software which continues to grow and refine as the conversation with the software continues - the brain is continuously engaged in the testing process and helps you to come up with new ideas and test cases to fulfill.

96: What is ad-hoc testing?

Answer:

Ad hoc testing is a commonly used term for software testing performed without planning and documentation (but can be applied to early scientific experimental studies). The tests are intended to be run only once, unless a defect is discovered. Ad hoc testing is a part of exploratory testing, being the least formal of test methods.

97: What are the benefits offered by exploratory testing?

Answer:

Below are described several benefits offered by exploratory testing:

a) Less preparation is needed
b) Important bugs are found quickly
c) The approach tends to be more intellectually stimulating than execution of scripted tests
d) Testers can use deductive reasoning based on the results of previous results to guide their future testing on the fly
e) Testers do not have to complete a current series of scripted tests before focusing in on or moving on to exploring a more target rich environment
f) After initial testing, most bugs are discovered by some sort of exploratory testing

98: What are the disadvantages that come with exploratory testing?

Answer:

One of the biggest disadvantages that come with exploratory testing is that tests invented and performed on the fly can't be reviewed in advance (and by that prevent errors in code and test cases), and that it can be difficult to show exactly which tests have been run. Anyway, this can be controlled with specific instruction to the tester, or by preparing automated tests where feasible.

99: What is the difference between assertion and functional testing?

Answer:

Assertion testing is performed at the API level and its purpose is to demonstrate that the code will perform as specified. Functional testing uses a high-level, building-block approach; it takes features that have been tested independently, assembles them into small applications and confirms that they work together.

100: What is a boundary condition?

Answer:

A boundary condition can be defined as a condition which occurs on the limits of the operation of the product, such as the largest or the most precise number, or the use of the product when environmental conditions are limited (such as running out of disk or memory). It is also known as a corner case condition.

101: What is data driven testing?

Answer:

Data driven testing is a scripting technique that stores test input and expected results in a table or spreadsheet, so that a single control script can execute all of the tests in the table.

Data driven testing is often used to support the application of test execution tools such as capture/playback tools.

102: What are the benefits of code-driven testing?

Answer:

Code driven test automation is a key feature of agile software development, where it is known as Test-driven development (TDD). The benefits of using code-driven testing are the following:

a) It is based on unit which are written to define the functionality before the code is written; only when all tests pass is the code considered complete
b) The code coverage is better
c) Because it is run constantly during development, the developer discovers defects immediately upon making a change, when it is least expensive to fix
d) Code refactoring is safer; transforming the code into a simpler form with less code duplication, but equivalent behavior, is much less likely to introduce new defects.

103: What is security testing?

Answer:

Security testing is a process to determine that an information system protects data and maintains functionality as intended. The six basic security concepts that need to be covered by security testing are: confidentiality, integrity, authentication, availability, authorization and non-repudiation.

104: What is the difference between authentication and authorization?

Answer:

Authentication is the process of establishing who the user is while authorization establishes what the user can do. Access control is an example of authorization.

105: Provide several examples of access control techniques.

Answer:

Access control techniques are sometimes categorized as either discretionary or non-discretionary. The three most widely recognized models are:

a) Discretionary Access Control (DAC)
b) Mandatory Access Control (MAC)
c) Role Based Access Control (RBAC).

106: Describe syntax testing.

Answer:

Syntax testing uses a model of the formally-defined syntax of the inputs to a component. The syntax is represented as a number of rules each of which defines the possible means of production of a symbol in terms of sequences of, iterations of, or selections between other symbols.

107: What is LCSAJ coverage?

Answer:

LCSAJ = Linear Code Sequence and Jump. It is defined by a triple, conventionally identified by line numbers in a source code listing, consisting of:

(the start of the linear code sequence, the end of the linear code sequence, the target line to which control flow is transferred).

As a formula,

LCSAJ coverage = executed LCSAJ sequences / total no. of LCSAJ sequences

108: What is basis path testing?

Answer:

Basis path testing is a white box test case design technique that uses the algorithmic flow of the program to design tests. It is actually a hybrid between path testing and branch testing.

109: What is backward compatibility testing?

Answer:

Backward compatibility testing is a type of testing that ensures that new version of the product continues to work with the assets created from older product. In cases where it is not possible to use assets created by older versions due to any reason, then proper migration path should be given to the user so that they can migrate smoothly from old version to new version.

110: What is upgrade testing?

Answer:

Upgrade testing is a testing technique that verifies if assets created with older versions can be used properly and that user's learning is not challenged. Old functionality should remain intact; it should not be dropped until unless there are business reasons to drop it.

111: What is benchmark testing? What are the characteristics of good benchmarks?

Answer:

Benchmark testing is a type of testing which is based on a repeatable environment so that the same test run under the same conditions will yield results that you can legitimately compare. Characteristics of good benchmarks (measurements) include:

a) Tests are repeatable.
b) Each iteration of a test starts in the same system state.
c) No other functions or applications are active in the system unless the scenario includes some amount of other activity going on in the system.

112: What is compatibility testing?

Answer:

Compatibility testing, part of software non-functional tests, is testing conducted on the application to evaluate the application's compatibility with the computing environment. Computing environment may contain some or all of the below mentioned elements:

a) Computing capacity of hardware platform
b) Bandwidth handling capacity of networking hardware
c) Compatibility of peripherals
d) Operating systems
e) Database
f) Other System Software

113: What is certification testing? What is the relation between certification and compatibility testing?

Answer:

Certification testing falls within the scope of compatibility testing. Product vendors run the complete suite of testing on the newer computing environment to get their application certified for a specific operating system or Database.

114: What is configuration testing?

Answer:

Configuration testing is the process of testing a system with each of the configurations of software and hardware that are supported. It is another variation on traditional performance testing. Rather than testing for performance from the perspective of load you are testing the effects of configuration changes in the application landscape on application performance and behavior.

115: What is Compliance testing?

Answer:

Compliance testing is a type of testing which checks whether the system was developed in accordance with standards, procedures and guidelines of Independent Organizations such as Federal Bureau, SEC (Securities Exchange Commission), ISO, HIPPA and so on.

116: What is agile testing?

Answer:

Agile testing is a software testing practice that follows the principles of agile software development. Agile testing does not emphasize testing procedures and focuses on foregoing testing against newly developed code until quality software from an end customer's perspective results.

117: What is exploratory testing?

Answer:

Exploratory testing is an approach to software testing that is concisely described as simultaneous learning, test design and test execution based on a quick test charter containing objectives and executed within delimited time-intervals. It uses structured approach to error guessing, based on experience, available defect data and domain expertise.

118: What is manual scripted testing?

Answer:

Manual scripted testing is the oldest and most rigorous type of software testing. In this particular type of testing, test cases are designed and reviewed by the team before executing it. There are many variation of this basic approach, test cases can be created at the basic functionality level or they can be created at the scenario level.

119: Which are the basic steps of the parallel testing?

Answer:

The steps that need to be performed on parallel testing are the following:

a) Reserve all inputs and outputs produced by the legacy system during selected pay cycles
b) Enter the reserved inputs into the new system once parallel testing starts
c) Run the tests in the new system over the inputted data
d) Finally, compare the outputs from the legacy system to the outputs from the new system.

120: What is penetration testing?

Answer:

Penetration testing is a testing method which evaluates the security of a computer system or network by simulating an attack from a malicious source. The process involves an active analysis of the system for any potential vulnerabilities that could result from poor or improper system configuration, both known and unknown hardware or software flaws, or operational weaknesses in process or technical countermeasures.

121: Give examples of web applications vulnerabilities.

Answer:

Web application can have a wide range of vulnerabilities. The most common are:

a) Technical vulnerabilities: URL manipulation, SQL injection, cross-site scripting, back-end authentication, password in memory, session hijacking, buffer overflow, web server configuration, credential management, click jacking
b) Business logic errors: Day-to-Day threat analysis, unauthorized logins, personal information modification, pricelist modification, unauthorized funds transfer, breach of customer trust etc

122: What is qualification testing?

Answer:

Qualification testing is a formally defined series of tests by which the functional, environmental, and reliability performance of a component or system may be evaluated in order to satisfy the engineer, contractor, or owner as to its satisfactory design and construction prior to final approval and acceptance.

123: What is recovery testing? Give examples of recovery testing scenarios.

Answer:

Recovery testing is the activity of testing how well an application is able to recover from crashes, hardware failures and other similar problems. It is the forced failure of the software in a variety of ways to verify that recovery is properly performed. Examples of recovery testing scenarios:

a) While an application is running, suddenly restart the computer, and afterwards check the validness of the application's data integrity.
b) While an application is receiving data from a network, unplug the connecting cable. After some time, plug the cable back in and analyze the application's ability to continue receiving data from the point at which the network connection disappeared.
c) Restart the system while a browser has a definite number of sessions. Afterwards, check that the browser is able to recover all of them.

124: What is the difference between recovery testing and reliability testing?

Answer:

Reliability testing tries to discover the specific point at which a failure occurs while recovery testing is done in order to check how fast and better the application can recover against any type of crash or hardware failure.

125: What is sanity testing?

Answer:

Sanity testing is a testing technique which determines if a new software version is performing well enough to accept it for a major testing effort.

126: What is the relation between smoke testing and sanity testing?

Answer:

Software sanity tests are commonly conflated with smoke tests. A smoke test determines whether it is possible to continue testing, as opposed to whether it is reasonable. A software smoke test determines whether the program launches and whether its interfaces are accessible and responsive. If the smoke test fails, it is impossible to conduct a sanity test.

127: What is scalability testing?

Answer:

Scalability testing is part of the battery of non-functional tests and represents the testing process of a software application for measuring its capability to scale up or scale out. It can determine the user load supported, the number of transactions, the data volume etc.

128: Give examples of several best practices used for creating scalable applications:

Answer:

Below are described several best practices used when dealing with scalable applications:

a) Use clustering technologies - network load balancing (NLB), cluster service, component load balancing (CLB)
b) Consider logical versus physical tiers
c) Isolate transactional methods - separate transactional methods from non transactional methods
d) Eliminate business logic layer state when possible

129: What is storage testing?

Answer:

Storage is the type of testing which verifies the program under test stores data files in the correct directories and that it reserves sufficient space to prevent unexpected termination resulting from lack of space. This is external storage as opposed to internal storage.

130: What is workflow testing?

Answer:

Workflow testing is a scripted end-to-end testing technique

which duplicates specific workflows which are expected to be utilized by the end-user.

131: What is model-based testing?

Answer:

Model-based testing is the application of Model based design for designing and executing the necessary artifacts to perform software testing. This is achieved by having a model that describes all aspects of the testing data, mainly the test cases and the test execution environment. Usually, the testing model is derived in whole or in part from a model that describes some (usually functional) aspects of the system under test.

132: What is mutation testing?

Answer:

Mutation testing is a method of software testing, which involves modifying programs' source code or byte code in small ways. In short, any tests which pass after code has been mutated are considered defective. These so-called mutations are based on well-defined mutation operators that either mimic typical programming errors (such as using the wrong operator or variable name) or force the creation of valuable tests (such as driving each expression to zero). The purpose is to help the tester develop effective tests or locate weaknesses in the test data used for the program or in sections of the code that are seldom or never accessed during execution.

133: What is the difference between mutation and fuzz testing?

Answer:

Fuzzing is a special area of mutation testing. In fuzzing, the messages or data exchanged inside communication interfaces (both inside and between software instances) are mutated, in order to catch failures or differences in processing the data.

134: Give examples of mutation operators for imperative languages.

Answer:

Below are some examples of mutation operators for imperative languages:

a) Statement deletion
b) Replace each Boolean sub-expression with true and false
c) Replace each arithmetic operation with another one, e.g. + with *, - and /
d) Replace each Boolean relation with another one, e.g. > with >=, == and <=
e) Replace each variable with another variable declared in the same scope (variable types should be the same)

135: What is operational testing? Give some pros and cons for performing it.

Answer:

Operational testing is the type of testing which is conducted to evaluate a system or component in its operational environment or an exact copy of the environment if the environment is in use with the live system. For any business critical system, operational testing should always take place. However, this type of testing is often difficult to fit into the development and testing lifecycle, as operational environment not available until very near the live date. It also may not be cost-effective or timely to conduct this type of test prior to going live.

136: What is orthogonal array testing?

Answer:

Orthogonal array testing is a systematic, statistical way of testing, based on orthogonal arrays. Orthogonal arrays can be applied in user interface testing, system testing, regression testing, configuration testing and performance testing.

137: What are the benefits of orthogonal array testing?

Answer:

The main benefits of orthogonal array testing are:

a) It provides uniformly distributed coverage of the test domain
b) Concise test set with fewer test cases is created
c) All pair-wise combinations of test set created
d) Arrives at complex combinations of all the variables
e) Simpler to generate and less error prone than test sets

created manually

f) Reduces testing cycle time

138: What is parallel testing?

Answer:

Parallel testing is a testing technique which has the purpose to ensure that a new application which has replaced its older version has been installed and is running correctly.

139: What is the purpose of impact analysis?

Answer:

The purpose of impact analysis is to determine how the existing system may be affected by changes. This helps to decide how much regression testing is necessary.

140: What is static testing? What are the benefits of performing reviews?

Answer:

Static testing is the process of testing a component or system at specification or implementation level without execution of that software, e.g. reviews (manual) or static code analysis (automated). Reviews are performed in order to identify errors as soon as possible in the development lifecycle; they offer the chance to find omissions and errors in the software specifications.

141: Which are the risks involved when performing static testing through reviews?

Answer:

The risks when performed reviews may include the following:

a) If misused they can lead to project team members frictions
b) The errors and omissions found should be regarded as a positive issue
c) The author should not take the errors and omissions personally
d) No follow up to is made to ensure correction has been made
e) Witch-hunts used when things are going wrong

142: What are the phases of a formal review?

Answer:

Formal review phases are the following:

a) Planning - define scope, select participants, allocate roles, define entry and exit criteria
b) Kick-off - distribute documents, explain objectives, process, check entry criteria
c) Individual preparation - each of participants studies the documents, takes notes, issues questions and comments
d) Review meeting - meeting participants discuss and log defects, make recommendations
e) Rework - fixing defects (by the author)

f) Follow-up - verify again, gather metrics, check exit criteria

143: What are the roles in a formal review?

Answer:

Formal reviews can use the following predefined roles:

a) Manager - schedules the review, monitor entry and exit criteria
b) Moderator - distributes the documents, leads the discussion, mediates various conflicting opinions
c) Author - owner of the deliverable to be reviewed
d) Reviewer - technical domain experts, identify and note findings
e) Scribe - records and documents the discussions during the meeting

144: Define the characteristics of a technical review.

Answer:

A technical review is a formal defect detection process which may vary in practice from quite informal to very formal. A technical review is usually led by a moderator, and the participating team includes also peers and technical domain experts. The main purpose of a technical review is to discuss, make decisions, evaluate alternatives, find defects, solve technical problems and check conformance to specifications and standards.

145: Which are the characteristics of inspection?

Answer:

Inspection is a formal process, based on checklists, entry and exit criteria. It has dedicated precise roles and is always led by the moderator. In inspection, metrics may be used but reports and list-of-findings are mandatory. It must have a follow-up process. Its main purpose is to find defects.

146: What is a walkthrough?

Answer:

A walkthrough is a formal process of inspecting algorithms and source code by following paths through the algorithms or code as determined by input conditions and choices made along the way. The author of the deliverable leads the review activity, others participate. Its main purposes are: learning, gaining understanding and defect finding.

147: What are the typical defects discovered while performing static analysis by tools?

Answer:

Typical defects discovered through static analysis by tools:

a) Reference to an un-initialized variable
b) Never used variables
c) Unreachable code
d) Programming standards violations
e) Security vulnerabilities

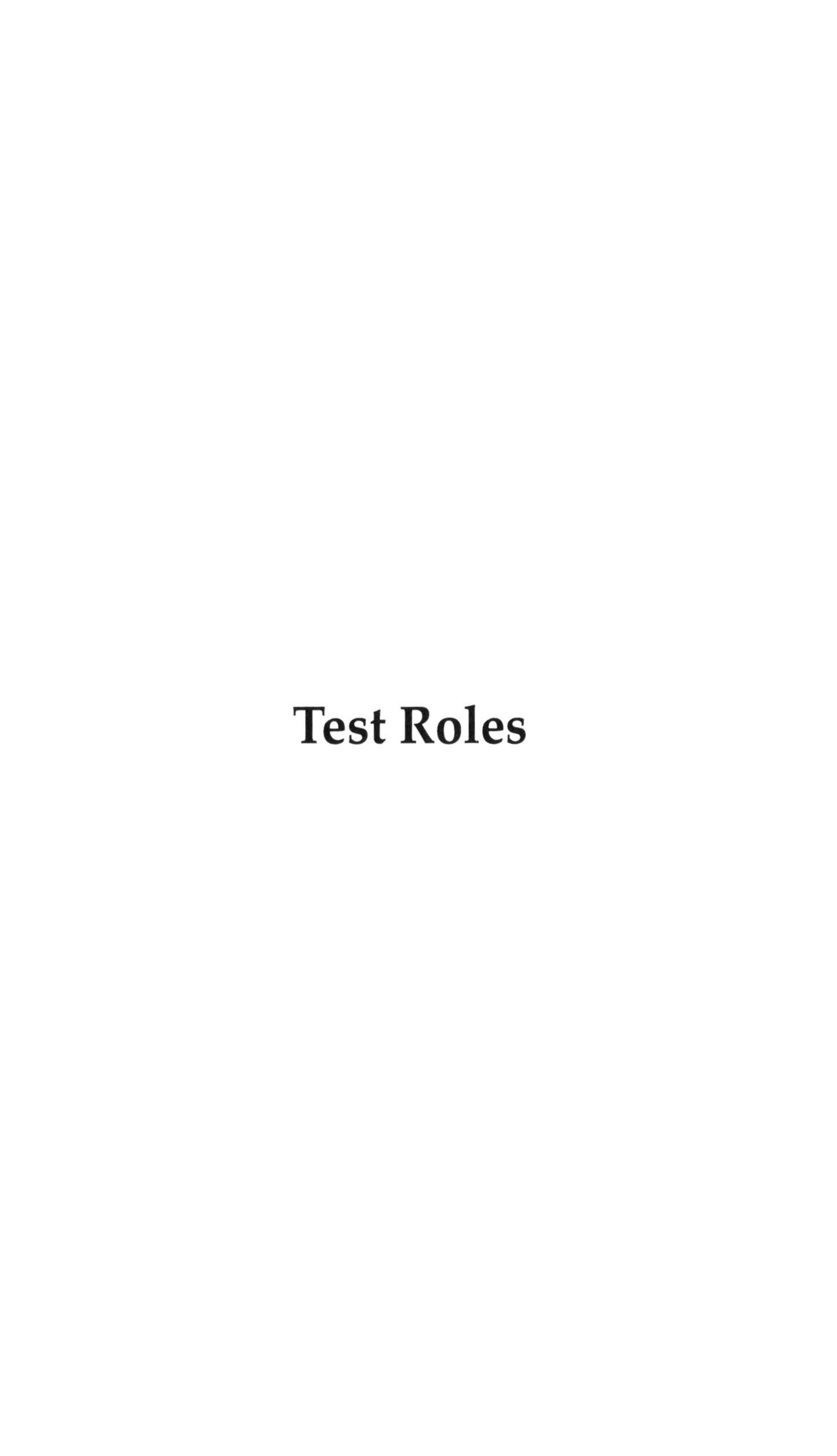

Test Roles

148: Which are the tasks executed by a test lead?

Answer:

A test lead:

a) Plans, estimates test effort, collaborates with project manager
b) Elaborates the test strategy
c) Initiate test specification, implementation and execution
d) Sets-up configuration management of test environment and deliverables
e) Monitors and controls the execution of tests
f) Chooses suitable test metrics
g) Decides if and to what degree to automate the tests
h) Selects tools
i) Schedules tests
j) Prepares summary test reports
k) Evaluates test measurements

149: Which are the tasks executed by a test analyst?

Answer:

A test analyst:

a) Identifies test objectives (targets)
b) Reviews product requirements and software specifications
c) Reviews test plans and test cases
d) Verifies requirements to test cases traceability
e) Defines test scenario details

f) Compares test results with test oracle

g) Assesses test risks

h) Gathers test measures

150: Which are the tasks executed by a test designer?

Answer:

A test designer:

a) Defines test approach (procedure)

b) Structures test implementation

c) Elaborates test case lists and writes main test cases

d) Assesses testability

e) Defines testing environment details

151: Which are the tasks executed by a tester?

Answer:

A tester:

a) Defines test approach (procedure)

b) Writes test cases

c) Reviews test cases (peer review)

d) Implements and executes tests

e) Records defects, prepares defect reports

152: What are the roles of a release manager?

Answer:

A release manager is:

a) Facilitator – serves as a liaison between varying

business units to guarantee smooth and timely delivery of software products or updates.

b) Gatekeeper – ‚holds the keys' to production systems/applications and takes responsibility for their implementations.

c) Architect – helps to identify, create and/or implement processes or products to efficiently manage the release of code.

d) Server Application Support Engineer – help troubleshoot problems with an application (although not typically at a code level).

e) Coordinator – utilized to coordinate disparate source trees, projects, teams and components

Test Management

153: What factors does the testing effort depend on?

Answer:

Testing effort depends on:

a) Product characteristics (complexity, specification)
b) Development process (team skills, tools, time factors
c) Defects discovered and rework involved
d) Failure risk of the product (likelihood, impact)

154: What is configuration management?

Answer:

Configuration management is a discipline applying technical and administrative direction and surveillance which:

a) Identifies the current configuration (hardware, software) in the life cycle of the system, together with any changes that are in course of being implemented.
b) Provides traceability of changes through the lifecycle of the system.
c) Permits the reconstruction of a system whenever necessary

155: What are the test approaches based on the point in time at which the bulk of the test design work is begun?

Answer:

There are two ways of classifying test approaches based on the point in time at which the bulk of the test design work is begun:

a) Preventative approaches, where tests are designed as early as possible.
b) Reactive approaches, where test design comes after the software or system has been produced

156: Which techniques can be used in order to identify risks?

Answer:

For both product and project risks, testers can identify risks through obe or more of the following techniques:

a) Expert interviews
b) Independent assessments
c) Use of risk templates
d) Lessons learned (e.g. project evaluation session)
e) Risk workshops
f) Brainstorming
g) Checklists
h) Calling on past experience

157: Which are the ways to handle an identified risk?

Answer:

Once a risk has been identified and analyzed, there are four possible ways to handle that risk:

a) Mitigate the risk through preventive measures to reduce likelihood and/or impact
b) Make contingency plans to reduce impact if the risk becomes an actuality

c) Transfer the risk to some other party to handle
d) Ignore and accept the risk

158: Enumerate and describe the bug relative severities.

Answer:

Below is the list of bugs relative severities, sorted in descending order:

a) Show stopper - it is impossible to continue with testing because of the severity of this error
b) Critical problem - testing can continue but we cannot go into production with this problem
c) Major problem - testing can continue but live this feature will cause severe disruption to business process in live operation
d) Medium problem - testing can continue and the system is likely to go live with only minimal departure from agreed business processes
e) Minor problem - both testing an live operations may progress. The problem should be corrected, but little or no changes to business processes are envisaged.
f) Cosmetic problem - e.g. colors, fonts, pitch size.

159: What is a bug tracker? Give examples of bug tracking systems.

Answer:

A bug tracker is a tracking system that is designed to manage software bus with computer programs. A major component of a bug tracking system is a database that records facts about known bugs. Facts may include the time a bug was reported, its severity, the erroneous program behavior, and details on how to reproduce the bug; as well as the identity of the person who reported it and any programmers who may be working on fixing it. Examples og bug tracking tools: Bugzilla, Mantis, Redmine, JIRA.

160: Which are the possible statuses of a bug?

Answer:

A bug can have one of the following statuses (the status may vary depending on the used bug tracking system)

a) New - when QA files new bug.
b) Deferred - if the bug is not related to current build or cannot be fixed in this release or bug is not important to fix immediately then the project manager can set the bug status as deferred.
c) Assigned - 'assigned to' field is set by project lead or manager and assigns bug to developer.
d) Resolved/Fixed - when developer makes necessary code changes and verifies the changes then he/she can make bug status as 'Fixed' and the bug is passed to testing team.
e) Not Reproducible - if the developer is not able to reproduce the bug by the steps given in bug report by

QA then developer can mark the bug as 'CNR'. QA needs action to check if bug is reproduced and can assign to developer with detailed reproducing steps.

f) Need more information -if the developer is not clear about the bug reproduce steps provided by QA to reproduce the bug

g) Reopen - if QA is not satisfied with the fix and if bug is still reproducible even after fix then QA can mark it as 'Reopen' so that developer can take appropriate action.

h) Closed - if bug is verified by the QA team and if the fix is ok and problem is solved then QA can mark bug as 'Closed'.

161: What is a PRD?

Answer:

PRD (product requirements document) is a high level description of the product (system), its intended use and the set of features it provides. It can be seen as a contract between, at a minimum, marketing and development describing completely and unambiguously the necessary attributes of the product to be developed.

162: Which are the typical components of a PRD?

Answer:

The typical components of a software product requirements document are:

a) Title & author Information
b) Purpose and scope, from both a technical and business perspective
c) Stakeholder identification
d) Market assessment and target demographics
e) Product overview and use cases
f) Requirements, including functional requirements (e.g. what a product should do), usability requirements, technical requirements (e.g. security, network, platform, integration, client), environmental requirements, support requirements, interaction requirements (e.g. how the software should work with other systems)
g) Constraints
h) High level workflow plans, timelines and milestones (more detail is defined through a project plan)
i) Evaluation plan and performance metrics

163: Which are the levels of requirements definitions?

Answer:

The levels of requirements definitions are:

a) MUST - This word "MUST", or the adjective ,REQUIRED'/ or "MANDATORY" means that the definition is an absolute requirement of the specification.
b) MUST NOT - This phrase means that the definition is an absolute prohibition of the specification.

c) SHOULD - The word "SHOULD", or the adjective ,DESIRABLE'/ means that there may exist valid reasons in particular circumstances to ignore this item, but the full implications must be understood and carefully weighed before choosing a different course.
d) MAY - The word "MAY" or the adjective ,OPTIONAL'/ means that this item is one of an allowed set of alternatives. An implementation that does not include this option MUST be prepared to inter-operate with another implementation that does include the option.

164: What is a MRD?

Answer:

A market requirements document (MRD) is a document that expresses the customer's wants and needs for the product or service. It is typically written as a part of product marketing or product management. The document should explain:

a) What (new) product is being discussed
b) Who the target customers are
c) What products are in competition with the proposed one
d) Why customers are likely to want this product

165: What is an URD?

Answer:

The user requirements document (URD) is a document usually

used in software engineering that specifies the requirements the user expects from software to be constructed in a software project. The URD can be used as a guide to planning cost, timetables, milestones, testing, etc. The explicit nature of the URD allows customers to show it to various stakeholders to make sure all necessary features are described.

166: What is a FRD?

Answer:

A functional requirement document (FRD) is a document usually used in software engineering that defines a function of a software system or its component. A function is described as a set of inputs, the behavior, and outputs.

Automation Testing

167: What is a capture and replay tool? What are the benefits of using such a tool?

Answer:

A capture and replay tool is a testing tool which enables test sessions to be recorded and then replayed. This has the following significant benefits:

a) The test sessions might be replayed at a later date with the confidence that the events can be reproduced
b) The test sessions might be edited and then replayed repeatedly or with several test sessions running at the same time (thus simulating additional load)
c) An enormous amount of effort is saved by re-using the test data without re-keying all the information

168: Give examples of several benefits of using automation tools in testing.

Answer:

The benefits of using automation tools in testing are the following:

a) Repetitive work is reduced (e.g. running regression tests, re-entering the same test data, and checking against coding standards).
b) Greater consistency and repeatability (e.g. tests executed by a tool, and tests derived from requirements).
c) Objective assessment (e.g. static measures, coverage

and system behavior).

d) Ease of access to information about tests or testing (e.g. statistics and graphs about test progress, incident rates and performance).

169: What is a test harness?

Answer:

A test harness or automated test framework is a collection of software and test data configured to test a program unit by running it under varying conditions and monitoring its behavior and outputs. It has two main parts: the test execution engine and the test script repository.

170: What are the objectives of a test harness?

Answer:

The objectives of a test harness are to:

a) Automate the testing process
b) Execute test suites of test cases
c) Generate associated test reports

171: What benefits provides the usage of a test harness?

Answer:

A test harness may provide some of the following benefits:

a) Increased productivity due to automation of the testing process.
b) Increased probability that regression testing will occur.

c) Increased quality of software components and application.
d) Ensure that subsequent test runs are exact duplicates of previous ones.
e) Testing can occur at times that the office is not staffed (i.e. at night)
f) A test script may include conditions and/or uses that are otherwise difficult to simulate (load, for example)

172: What is test automation? What are the approaches to test automation?

Answer:

Test automation is the use of software to control the execution of tests, the comparison of actual outcomes to predicted outcomes, the setting up of test preconditions, and other test control and test reporting functions. There are two general approaches to test automation:

a) Code-driven testing - the public interfaces to classes, modules, or libraries are tested with a variety of input arguments to validate that the results that are returned are correct.
b) Graphical user interface testing - a testing framework generates user interface events such as keystrokes and mouse clicks, and observes the changes that result in the user interface, to validate that the observable behavior of the program is correct.

173: Describe the categories of automation testing frameworks (based on the automation component they leverage)

Answer:

Automation testing frameworks can be divided into five categories, based of the automation component they leverage. These categories are:

a) Data-driven testing
b) Modularity-driven testing
c) Keyword-driven testing
d) Hybrid testing
e) Model-based testing

174: Give examples of several test automation tools.

Answer:

Below are several tools used in automation testing:

a) HP QuickTest Professional (provided by HP)
b) IBM Rational Functional Tester (provided by IBM Rational)
c) Parasoft SOAtest (provided by Parasoft)
d) Rational robot (provided by IBM Rational)
e) Selenium
f) SilkTest
g) TestComplete
h) TestPartner
i) Visual Studio Test Professional

j) WATIR
k) JMeter

175: What is code coverage?

Answer:

Code coverage is a measure used in software testing which describes the degree to which the source code of a program has been tested. It is a form of testing that inspects the code directly and is therefore a form of white box testing.

176: Which are the main coverage criteria?

Answer:

The main code coverage criteria are the following:

a) Function coverage - Has each function (or subroutine) in the program been called?
b) Statement coverage - Has each node in the program been executed?
c) Decision coverage or branch coverage - Has every edge in the program been executed? For instance, have the requirements of each branch of each control structure (such as in IF and CASE statements) been met as well as not met?
d) Condition coverage (or predicate coverage) - Has each boolean sub-expression evaluated both to true and false? This does not necessarily imply decision coverage.

e) Condition/decision coverage - Both decision and condition coverage should be satisfied.

177: Give examples of code coverage tools used in software testing:

Answer:

Below are stated several code coverage tools, divided on programming language they can be used to:

a) c++ - Insure++, Tessy, Testwell CTC++, Trucov
b) C# .NET - NCover, Testwell CTC++
c) Java - Clover, Cobertura, EMMA, Jtest, Serenity, Testwell CTC++
d) PHP - PHPUnit, also need Xdebug to make coverage reports

178: What is build automation?

Answer:

Build automation is the act of scripting or automating a wide variety of tasks that software developers do in their day-to-day activities including things like:

a) Compiling computer source code into binary code
b) Packaging binary code
c) Running tests
d) Deployment to production systems
e) Creating documentation and/or release notes

179: What is continuous integration? Give examples of continuous integration tools.

Answer:

Continuous integration implements continuous processes of applying quality control – small pieces of effort, applied frequently. Continuous integration aims to improve the quality of software, and to reduce the time taken to deliver it, by replacing the traditional practice of applying quality control after completing all development. Examples of continuous integration tools: Apache Continuum, Automated Build Studio, BuildBot, CruiseControl, Hudson, Rational Team Concert and so on.

180: What are the advantages of using continuous integration tools?

Answer:

Continuous integration has many advantages:

a) When unit tests fail or a bug emerges, developers might revert the codebase back to a bug-free state, without wasting time debugging
b) Developers detect and fix integration problems continuously - avoiding last-minute chaos at release dates, (when everyone tries to check in their slightly incompatible versions).
c) Early warning of broken/incompatible code
d) Early warning of conflicting changes

e) Immediate unit testing of all changes
f) Constant availability of a "current" build for testing, demo, or release purposes
g) Immediate feedback to developers on the quality, functionality, or system-wide impact of code they are writing
h) Frequent code check-in pushes developers to create modular, less complex code
i) Metrics generated from automated testing and CI (such as metrics for code coverage, code complexity, and features complete) focus developers on developing functional, quality code, and help develop momentum in a team

181: What are the disadvantages of using continuous integration tools?

Answer:

Many teams using continuous integration report that the advantages outweigh the disadvantages. The effect of finding and fixing integration bugs early in the development process saves both time and money over the lifespan of a project. The disadvantages would be:

a) Initial setup time required
b) Well-developed test-suite required to achieve automated testing advantages
c) Large-scale refactoring can be troublesome due to

continuously changing code base

d) Hardware costs for build machines can be significant

Software Development Process

182: Which are the activity mappings in the V testing model?

Answer:

V testing model implies the following activity mappings:

a) Requirements - Acceptance testing
b) Specification - System testing
c) Architectural design - Integration testing
d) Detailed design - Unit testing
e) Coding

183: Which test levels are usually included in the common type of V-model?

Answer:

The test levels included into V-model are component testing, integration testing, system testing and acceptance testing.

184: What is a software development process? Give example of several software development models.

Answer:

A software development process, also known as a software development lifecycle, is a structure imposed on the development of a software product. The most well known software development models are:

a) Waterfall model - after each phase is finished, it proceeds to the next one.
b) Spiral model - risk management at regular stages in the development cycle

c) Iterative and Incremental development - prescribes the construction of initially small but ever larger portions of a software project to help all those involved to uncover important issues early before problems or faulty assumptions can lead to disaster
d) Agile development - uses iterative development as a basis but advocates a lighter and more people-centric viewpoint than traditional approaches

185: What are phases of the waterfall development model?

Answer:

The waterfall model development phases are the following:

a) Requirements specification (Requirements analysis)
b) Software Design
c) Integration
d) Testing (or Validation)
e) Deployment (or Installation)
f) Maintenance

186: Which are the weaknesses of waterfall development model?

Answer:

One major Waterfall flaw is that the entire software product is being worked on at one time and there is no way to partition the system for delivery of pieces of the system. Other weaknesses would be:

a) It is linear - any attempt to go back two or more phases to correct a problem or deficiency results in major increases in cost and schedule
b) Integration problems usually surface too late; previously undetected errors or design deficiencies will emerge, adding risk with little time to recover
c) Users can't see quality until the end
d) Deliverables are created for each phase and are considered frozen. If the deliverable of a phase changes, which often happens, the project will suffer schedule problems

187: Describe spiral development model.

Answer:

The Spiral development model is visualized as a process passing through some number of iterations, with the four quadrant diagram representative of the following activities:

a) formulate plans to: identify software targets, selected to implement the program, clarify the project development restrictions
b) Risk analysis: an analytical assessment of selected programs, to consider how to identify and eliminate risk
c) the implementation of the project: the implementation of software development and verification

188: What are the weaknesses of the spiral development model?

Answer:

The model is complex, and developers, managers, and customers may find it too complicated to use. Other specific weaknesses would be:

a) Considerable risk assessment expertise is required
b) Hard to define objective, verifiable milestones that indicate readiness to proceed through the next iteration
c) May be expensive - time spent planning, resetting objectives, doing risk analysis, and prototyping may be excessive

189: Describe on short the incremental development model.

Answer:

Incremental development model is at the heart of a cyclic software development process developed in response to the weaknesses of the waterfall model. It starts with an initial planning and ends with deployment with the cyclic interactions in between. Iterative and incremental development are essential parts of the Rational Unified Process, Extreme Programming and generally the various agile software development frameworks. It follows a similar process to the plan-do-check-act cycle of business process improvement.

190: What are the weaknesses of the incremental

development model?

Answer:

Incremental development model has several flaws:

a) Definition of a complete, fully functional system must be done early in the life cycle to allow for the definition of the increments
b) The model does not allow for iterations within each increment
c) Because some modules will be completed long before others, well-defined interfaces are required
d) Requires good planning and design: Management must take care to distribute the work; the technical staff must watch dependencies

191: Give examples of several principles which underlie the Agile Manifesto.

Answer:

There are twelve principles which underlie the Agile Manifesto, which include:

a) Customer satisfaction by rapid delivery of useful software
b) Welcome changing requirements, even late in development
c) Working software is delivered frequently (weeks rather than months)
d) Working software is the principal measure of progress

e) Sustainable development, able to maintain a constant pace
f) Close, daily co-operation between business people and developers
g) Face-to-face conversation is the best form of communication (co-location)
h) Projects are built around motivated individuals, who should be trusted
i) Continuous attention to technical excellence and good design
j) Simplicity
k) Self-organizing teams
l) Regular adaptation to changing circumstances

192: Describe software development's life cycle.

Answer:

There are four main phases in a software development life cycle:

a) Pre-alpha - refers to all activities performed during the software project prior to testing. These activities can include requirements analysis, software design, software development and unit testing.
b) Alpha - alpha phase of the release life cycle is the first phase to begin software testing. It usually ends with a feature freeze, indicating that no more features will be added to the software. At this time, the software is said

to be feature complete.

c) Beta - the focus of beta testing is reducing impacts to users, often incorporating usability testing. The process of delivering a beta version to the users is called beta release and this is typically the first time that the software is available outside of the organization that developed it.
d) Release candidate - a version with potential to be a final product, ready to release unless fatal bugs emerge. In this stage of product stabilization, all product features have been designed, coded and tested through one or more beta cycles with no known showstopper-class bug.

193: What is the difference between open and closed beta?

Answer:

Closed beta versions are released to a select group of individuals for a user test, while open betas are to a larger community group, sometimes to anybody interested. The testers report any bugs that they find, and sometimes suggest additional features they think should be available in the final version.

194: What is GA (in terms of software)?

Answer:

General availability or general acceptance (GA) is the point where all necessary commercialization activities have been completed and the software has been made available to the general market either via the web or physical media.

195: What is software versioning?

Answer:

Software versioning is the process of assigning either unique version names or unique version numbers to unique states of computer software. Within a given version number category (major, minor), these numbers are generally assigned in increasing order and correspond to new developments in the software. At a fine-grained level, revision control is often used for keeping track of incrementally different versions of electronic information, whether or not this information is actually computer software.

196: What is code review?

Answer:

Code review is systematic examination (often as peer review) of computer source code. It is intended to find and fix mistakes overlooked in the initial development phase, improving both the overall quality of software and the developers' skills. Reviews are done in various forms such as pair programming, informal walkthroughs, and formal inspections.

Project Management

197: What is project management?

Answer:

Project management is the discipline of planning, organizing, securing and managing resources to bring about the successful completion of specific project goals and objectives. It is sometimes conflated with program management, however technically that is actually a higher level construction: a group of related and somehow interdependent engineering projects.

198: What are the steps that are completed in a traditional project management phased approach?

Answer:

A traditional phased approach identifies 5 phases in the development of a project:

a) Project initiation stage;
b) Project planning and design stage;
c) Project execution and construction stage;
d) Project monitoring and controlling systems;
e) Project completion.

199: What is CCPM?

Answer:

Critical Chain Project Management (CCPM) is a method of planning and managing projects that puts more emphasis on the resources (physical and human) needed in order to execute project tasks. The most complex part involves engineering professionals of different fields working together. The goal is to increase the rate of throughput (or completion rates) of projects in an organization.

200: What is event chain methodology?

Answer:

Event chain methodology is another method that complements critical path method and critical chain project management methodologies. It is based on the following principles.

a) *Probabilistic moment of risk* - tasks are affected by external events, which can occur at some point in the middle of the task
b) *Event chains* - events can cause other events, which will create event chains. These event chains can significantly affect the course of the project
c) *Critical events or event chains* - the single events or the event chains that have the most potential to affect the projects are the 'critical events' or 'critical chains of events'
d) *Project tracking with events* - even if a project is partially completed and data about the project duration, cost, and events occurred is available, it is still possible to refine information about future potential events and helps to forecast future project performance
e) *Event chain visualization* - events and event chains can be visualized using event chain diagrams on a Gantt chart

This page is intentionally left blank

HR Questions

Review these typical interview questions and think about how you would answer them. Read the answers listed; you will find best possible answers along with strategies and suggestions.

1: Tell me about yourself?

Answer:

The most often asked question in interviews. You need to have a short statement prepared in your mind. Keep your answer to one or two minutes. Don't ramble. Be careful that it does not sound rehearsed. Limit it to work-related items unless instructed otherwise. Talk about things you have done and jobs you have held that relate to the position you are interviewing for. Start with the item farthest back and work up to the present (If you have a profile or personal statement(s) at the top of your CV use this as your starting point).

2: Why did you leave your last job?

Answer:

Stay positive regardless of the circumstances. Never refer to a major problem with management and never speak ill of supervisors, co- workers or the organization. If you do, you will be the one looking bad. Keep smiling and talk about leaving for a positive reason such as an opportunity, a chance to do something special or other forward- looking reasons.

3: What experience do you have in this field?

Answer:

Speak about specifics that relate to the position you are applying for. If you do not have specific experience, get as close as you can.

4: Do you consider yourself successful?

Answer:

You should always answer yes and briefly explain why. A good explanation is that you have set goals, and you have met some and are on track to achieve the others.

5: What do co-workers say about you?

Answer:

Be prepared with a quote or two from co-workers. Either a specific statement or a paraphrase will work. Bill Smith, a co-worker at Clarke Company, always said I was the hardest worker's he had ever known. It should be as powerful as Bill having said it at the interview herself.

6: What do you know about this organization?

Answer:

This question is one reason to do some research on the organization before the interview. Research the company's products, size, reputation, Image, goals, problems, management style, skills, History and philosophy. Be informed and interested. Find out where they have been and where they are going. What are the current issues and who are the major players?

7: What have you done to improve your knowledge in the last year?

Answer:

Try to include improvement activities that relate to the job. A wide variety of activities can be mentioned as positive self-improvement. Have some good ones handy to mention.

8: Are you applying for other jobs?

Answer:

Be honest but do not spend a lot of time in this area. Keep the focus on this job and what you can do for this organization. Anything else is a distraction.

9: Why do you want to work for this organization?

Answer:

This may take some thought and certainly, should be based on the research you have done on the organization. Sincerity is extremely important here and will easily be sensed. Relate it to your long-term career goals. Never talk about what you want; first talk about their Needs. You want to be part of an exciting forward-moving company. You can make a definite contribution to specific company goals.

10: Do you know anyone who works for us?

Answer:

Be aware of the policy on relatives working for the organization. This can affect your answer even though they asked about friends not relatives. Be careful to mention a friend only if they are well thought of.

11: What kind of salary do you need?

Answer:

A loaded question! A nasty little game that you will probably lose if you answer first. So, do not answer it. Instead, say something like/ that's a tough question. Can you tell me the range for this position? In most cases, the interviewer, taken off guard, will tell you. If not, say that it can depend on the details of the job. Then give a wide range.

12: Are you a team player?

Answer:

You are, of course, a team player. Be sure to have examples ready. Specifics that show you often perform for the good of the team rather than for yourself is good evidence of your team attitude. Do not brag; just say it in a matter-of-fact tone. This is a key point.

13: How long would you expect to work for us if hired?

Answer:

Specifics here are not good. Something like this should work: I'd like it to be a long time. Or As long as we both feel I'm doing a good job.

14: Have you ever had to fire anyone? How did you feel about

that?

Answer:

This is serious. Do not make light of it or in any way seem like you like to fire people. At the same time, you will do it when it is the right thing to do. When it comes to the organization versus the individual who has created a harmful situation, you will protect the organization. Remember firing is not the same as layoff or reduction in force.

15: What is your philosophy towards work?

Answer:

The interviewer is not looking for a long or flowery dissertation here. Do you have strong feelings that the job gets done? Yes. That's the type of answer that works best here. Keep it short and positive, showing a benefit to the organization.

16: If you had enough money to retire right now, would you?

Answer:

Answer yes if you would. But since you need to work, this is the type of work you prefer. Do not say yes if you do not mean it.

17: Have you ever been asked to leave a position?

Answer:

If you have not, say no. If you have, be honest, brief and avoid saying negative things about the people or organization involved.

18: Explain how you would be an asset to this organization.

Answer:

You should be anxious for this question. It gives you a chance to highlight your best points as they relate to the position being discussed. Give a little advance thought to this relationship.

19: Why should we hire you?

Answer:

Point out how your assets meet what the organization needs. Also mention about your knowledge, experience, abilities, and skills. Never mention any other candidates to make a comparison.

20: Tell me about a suggestion you have made.

Answer:

Have a good one ready. Be sure and use a suggestion that was accepted and was then considered successful. One related to the type of work applied for is a real plus.

21: What irritates you about co-workers?

Answer:

This is a trap question. Think real hard but fail to come up with anything that irritates you. A short statement that you seem to get along with folks is great.

22: What is your greatest strength?

Answer:

Numerous answers are good, just stay positive. A few good examples: Your ability to prioritize, Your problem-solving skills, Your ability to work under pressure, Your ability to focus on projects, Your professional expertise, Your leadership skills, Your positive attitude

23: Tell me about your dream job or what are you looking for in a job?

Answer:

Stay away from a specific job. You cannot win. If you say the job you are contending for is it, you strain credibility. If you say another job is it, you plant the suspicion that you will be dissatisfied with this position if hired. The best is to stay genetic and say something like: A job where I love the work, like the people, can contribute and can't wait to get to work.

24: Why do you think you would do well at this job?

Answer:

Give several reasons and include skills, experience and interest.

25: What do you find the most attractive about this position (Least attractive)?

Answer:

- **a)** List a couple of attractive factors such as the

responsibility the post offers and the opportunity to work with experienced teams that have a reputation for innovation and creativity.

b) Say you'd need more information and time before being able to make a judgment on any unattractive aspects.

26: What kind of person would you refuse to work with?

Answer:

Do not be trivial. It would take disloyalty to the organization, violence or lawbreaking to get you to object. Minor objections will label you as a whiner.

27: What is more important to you: the money or the work?

Answer:

Money is always important, but the work is the most important. There is no better answer.

28: What would your previous supervisor say your strongest point is?

Answer:

There are numerous good possibilities: Loyalty, Energy, Positive attitude, Leadership, Team player, Expertise, Initiative, Patience, Hard work, Creativity, Problem solver.

29: Tell me about a problem you had with a supervisor.

Answer:

Biggest trap of all! This is a test to see if you will speak ill of your boss. If you fall for it and tell about a problem with a former boss, you may well below the interview right there. Stay positive and develop a poor memory about any trouble with a supervisor.

30: What has disappointed you about a job?

Answer:

Don't get trivial or negative. Safe areas are few but can include: Not enough of a challenge. You were laid off in a reduction Company did not win a contract, which would have given you more responsibility.

31: Tell me about your ability to work under pressure.

Answer:

You may say that you thrive under certain types of pressure. Give an example that relates to the type of position applied for.

32: Do your skills match this job or another job more closely?

Answer:

Probably this one! Do not give fuel to the suspicion that you may want another job more than this one.

33: What motivates you to do your best on the job?

Answer:

This is a personal trait that only you can say, but good

examples are: Challenge, Achievement, and Recognition.

34: Are you willing to work overtime? Nights? Weekends?

Answer:

This is up to you. Be totally honest.

35: How would you know you were successful on this job?

Answer:

Several ways are good measures: You set high standards for yourself and meet them. Your outcomes are a success. Your boss tells you that you are successful and doing a great job.

36: Would you be willing to relocate if required?

Answer:

You should be clear on this with your family prior to the interview if you think there is a chance it may come up. Do not say yes just to get the job if the real answer is no. This can create a lot of problems later on in your career. Be honest at this point. This will save you from future grief.

37: Are you willing to put the interests of the organization ahead of your own?

Answer:

This is a straight loyalty and dedication question. Do not worry about the deep ethical and philosophical implications. Just say yes.

38: Describe your management style.

Answer:

Try to avoid labels. Some of the more common labels, like progressive, salesman or consensus, can have several meanings or descriptions depending on which management expert you listen to. The situational style is safe, because it says you will manage according to the situation, instead of one size fits all.

39: What have you learned from mistakes on the job?

Answer:

Here you have to come up with something or you strain credibility. Make it small, well intentioned mistake with a positive lesson learned. An example would be, working too far ahead of colleagues on a project and thus throwing coordination off.

40: Do you have any blind spots?

Answer:

Trick question! If you know about blind spots, they are no longer blind spots. Do not reveal any personal areas of concern here. Let them do their own discovery on your bad points. Do not hand it to them.

41: If you were hiring a person for this job, what would you look for?

Answer:

Be careful to mention traits that are needed and that you have.

42: Do you think you are overqualified for this position?

Answer:

Regardless of your qualifications, state that you are very well qualified for the position you've been interviewed for.

43: How do you propose to compensate for your lack of experience?

Answer:

First, if you have experience that the interviewer does not know about, bring that up: Then, point out (if true) that you are a hard working quick learner.

44: What qualities do you look for in a boss?

Answer:

Be generic and positive. Safe qualities are knowledgeable, a sense of humor, fair, loyal to subordinates and holder of high standards. All bosses think they have these traits.

45: Tell me about a time when you helped resolve a dispute between others.

Answer:

Pick a specific incident. Concentrate on your problem solving technique and not the dispute you settled.

46: What position do you prefer on a team working on a project?

Answer:

Be honest. If you are comfortable in different roles, point that out.

47: Describe your work ethic.

Answer:

Emphasize benefits to the organization. Things like, determination to get the job done and work hard but enjoy your work are good.

48: What has been your biggest professional disappointment?

Answer:

Be sure that you refer to something that was beyond your control. Show acceptance and no negative feelings.

49: Tell me about the most fun you have had on the job.

Answer:

Talk about having fun by accomplishing something for the organization.

50: What would you do for us? (What can you do for us that someone else can't?)

a) Relate past experiences that represent success in Working for your previous employer.

b) Talk about your fresh perspective and the relevant experience you can bring to the company.
c) Highlight your track record of providing creative, Workable solutions.

51: Do you have any questions for me?

Answer:

Always have some questions prepared. Questions prepared where you will be an asset to the organization are good. How soon will I be able to be productive? What type of projects will I be able to assist on?

And Finally Good Luck!

INDEX

Software Testing Questions

General Testing Concepts

Testing Phases

33: Which are the phases of test planning?
34: What tasks are implemented through test control?
35: Which factors must be taken into account when choosing a specific testing technique?
36: Which are the steps that need to be performed during test implementation?
37: What are the activities performed during test execution?
38: What are the reasons to prioritize the test cases?
39: Give example of several test cases prioritization criteria:
40: What needs to be taken into account when evaluating the exit criteria?
41: What should include a test summary report?
42: What are the processes implemented during test closure activity?
43: Give examples of several best practices in preparing manual test scripts.

Types Of Testing

44: What is verification? In which testing levels is it most used?
45: What is validation? In which testing levels is it most used?
46: What is unit testing? By whom is it usually performed?
47: What are the benefits offered by unit testing?
48: What is integration testing?
49: What are the integration testing strategies?
50: What is a driver? In which type of testing is it used?
51: What is a stub? In which type of testing is it used?
52: What is system testing?
53: What is acceptance testing?
54: Which are the main goals of acceptance testing?
55: Which are the typical forms of acceptance testing?
56: Which is the difference between Alpha and Beta testing?
57: What is functional testing?
58: What is non-functional testing? Give several examples.
59: What is usability testing?
60: What is installability testing?
61: What is load testing?
62: What is the difference between stress testing and performance testing?
63: What is performance testing? Which are its sub-genres?
64: Which are the activities involved by performance testing?
65: Give several reasons why stress testing is necessary.
66: Which is the relationship between stress testing and branch coverage?
67: What is structural testing?
68: What is confirmation testing?
69: What is the difference between confirmation testing and debugging?
70: What is regression testing?

71: Define maintenance testing and give example of some operations included into it.
72: Describe equivalence partitioning testing technique. Provide a short example.
73: What is all-pairs testing (or pairwise testing)?
74: Describe boundary value analysis technique. Provide a short example.
75: What is context-driven testing?
76: What is conversion testing?
77: What is destructive software testing?
78: What is dependency testing?
79: What is dynamic testing? Give example of several dynamic testing methodologies.
80: What is domain testing?
81: What is error-handling testing?
82: What is end to end testing?
83: What is fuzz testing?
84: Which are the types of bugs found through fuzz testing?
85: What is gray box testing?
86: What is the goal of globalization testing?
87: What type of tests does globalization testing include?
88: What is internationalization testing?
89: Which are the tasks involved by internationalization process?
90: What is localization testing?
91: What is inter-system testing?
92: What is loop testing?
93: What is accessibility testing?
94: Give examples of some typical test cases for accessibility testing.
95: What is the difference between active and passive testing?
96: What is ad-hoc testing?
97: What are the benefits offered by exploratory testing?
98: What are the disadvantages that come with exploratory testing?
99: What is the difference between assertion and functional testing?
100: What is a boundary condition?
101: What is data driven testing?
102: What are the benefits of code-driven testing?
103: What is security testing?
104: What is the difference between authentication and authorization?
105: Provide several examples of access control techniques.
106: Describe syntax testing.
107: What is LCSAJ coverage?
108: What is basis path testing?
109: What is backward compatibility testing?
110: What is upgrade testing?
111: What is benchmark testing? What are the characteristics of good benchmarks?
112: What is compatibility testing?

113: What is certification testing? What is the relation between certification and compatibility testing?
114: What is configuration testing?
115: What is Compliance testing?
116: What is agile testing?
117: What is exploratory testing?
118: What is manual scripted testing?
119: Which are the basic steps of the parallel testing?
120: What is penetration testing?
121: Give examples of web applications vulnerabilities.
122: What is qualification testing?
123: What is recovery testing? Give examples of recovery testing scenarios.
124: What is the difference between recovery testing and reliability testing?
125: What is sanity testing?
126: What is the relation between smoke testing and sanity testing?
127: What is scalability testing?
128: Give examples of several best practices used for creating scalable applications:
129: What is storage testing?
130: What is workflow testing?
131: What is model-based testing?
132: What is mutation testing?
133: What is the difference between mutation and fuzz testing?
134: Give examples of mutation operators for imperative languages.
135: What is operational testing? Give some pros and cons for performing it.
136: What is orthogonal array testing?
137: What are the benefits of orthogonal array testing?
138: What is parallel testing?
139: What is the purpose of impact analysis?
140: What is static testing? What are the benefits of performing reviews?
141: Which are the risks involved when performing static testing through reviews?
142: What are the phases of a formal review?
143: What are the roles in a formal review?
144: Define the characteristics of a technical review.
145: Which are the characteristics of inspection?
146: What is a walkthrough?
147: What are the typical defects discovered while performing static analysis by tools?

Test Roles

148: Which are the tasks executed by a test lead?
149: Which are the tasks executed by a test analyst?
150: Which are the tasks executed by a test designer?
151: Which are the tasks executed by a tester?

152: What are the roles of a release manager?

Test Management

153: What factors does the testing effort depend on?

154: What is configuration management?

155: What are the test approaches based on the point in time at which the bulk of the test design work is begun?

156: Which techniques can be used in order to identify risks?

157: Which are the ways to handle an identified risk?

158: Enumerate and describe the bug relative severities.

159: What is a bug tracker? Give examples of bug tracking systems.

160: Which are the possible statuses of a bug?

161: What is a PRD?

162: Which are the typical components of a PRD?

163: Which are the levels of requirements definitions?

164: What is a MRD?

165: What is an URD?

166: What is a FRD?

Automation Testing

167: What is a capture and replay tool? What are the benefits of using such a tool?

168: Give examples of several benefits of using automation tools in testing.

169: What is a test harness?

170: What are the objectives of a test harness?

171: What benefits provides the usage of a test harness?

172: What is test automation? What are the approaches to test automation?

173: Describe the categories of automation testing frameworks (based on the automation component they leverage)

174: Give examples of several test automation tools.

175: What is code coverage?

176: Which are the main coverage criteria?

177: Give examples of code coverage tools used in software testing:

178: What is build automation?

179: What is continuous integration? Give examples of continuous integration tools.

180: What are the advantages of using continuous integration tools?

181: What are the disadvantages of using continuous integration tools?

Software Development Process

182: Which are the activity mappings in the V testing model?

183: Which test levels are usually included in the common type of V-model?

184: What is a software development process? Give example of several software development models.

185: What are phases of the waterfall development model?

186: Which are the weaknesses of waterfall development model?

187: Describe spiral development model.

188: What are the weaknesses of the spiral development model?

189: Describe on short the incremental development model.

190: What are the weaknesses of the incremental development model?

191: Give examples of several principles which underlie the Agile Manifesto.

192: Describe software development's life cycle.

193: What is the difference between open and closed beta?

194: What is GA (in terms of software)?

195: What is software versioning?

196: What is code review?

Project Management

197: What is project management?

198: What are the steps that are completed in a traditional project management phased approach?

199: What is CCPM?

200: What is event chain methodology?

HR Questions

1: Tell me about yourself?
2: Why did you leave your last job?
3: What experience do you have in this field?
4: Do you consider yourself successful?
5: What do co-workers say about you?
6: What do you know about this organization?
7: What have you done to improve your knowledge in the last year?
8: Are you applying for other jobs?
9: Why do you want to work for this organization?
10: Do you know anyone who works for us?
11: What kind of salary do you need?
12: Are you a team player?
13: How long would you expect to work for us if hired?
14: Have you ever had to fire anyone? How did you feel about that?
15: What is your philosophy towards work?
16: If you had enough money to retire right now, would you?
17: Have you ever been asked to leave a position?
18: Explain how you would be an asset to this organization.
19: Why should we hire you?
20: Tell me about a suggestion you have made.
21: What irritates you about co-workers?
22: What is your greatest strength?
23: Tell me about your dream job or what are you looking for in a job?
24: Why do you think you would do well at this job?
25: What do you find the most attractive about this position? (Least attractive?)
26: What kind of person would you refuse to work with?
27: What is more important to you: the money or the work?
28: What would your previous supervisor say your strongest point is?
29: Tell me about a problem you had with a supervisor.
30: What has disappointed you about a job?
31: Tell me about your ability to work under pressure.
32: Do your skills match this job or another job more closely?
33: What motivates you to do your best on the job?
34: Are you willing to work overtime? Nights? Weekends?
35: How would you know you were successful on this job?
36: Would you be willing to relocate if required?
37: Are you willing to put the interests of the organization ahead of your own?
38: Describe your management style.
39: What have you learned from mistakes on the job?
40: Do you have any blind spots?

41: If you were hiring a person for this job, what would you look for?

42: Do you think you are overqualified for this position?

43: How do you propose to compensate for your lack of experience?

44: What qualities do you look for in a boss?

45: Tell me about a time when you helped resolve a dispute between others.

46: What position do you prefer on a team working on a project?

47: Describe your work ethic.

48: What has been your biggest professional disappointment?

49: Tell me about the most fun you have had on the job.

50: What would you do for us? (What can you do for us that someone else can't?)

51: Do you have any questions for me?

Some of the following titles might also be handy:

Made in the USA
Lexington, KY
13 July 2011